Maybe You Can't

Ed Reynolds
Jeff VanderHorst

Charleston, SC
www.PalmettoPublishing.com

Maybe You Can't
Text copyright © 2019 by Ed Reynolds and Jeff VanderHorst
Illustrations copyright © 2019 by Celeste Bergman

All rights reserved

No portion of this book may be reproduced, stored in a retrieval system, or transmitted in any form by any means–electronic, mechanical, photocopy, recording, or other–except for brief quotations in printed reviews, without prior permission of the author.

First Edition

Paperback ISBN: 978-1-64990-557-4

Your whole life is in front of you. There are so many career paths to pursue and maybe yours will be exciting and financially rewarding!

However, there are times things don't always turn out as planned!

Here are some possibilities...

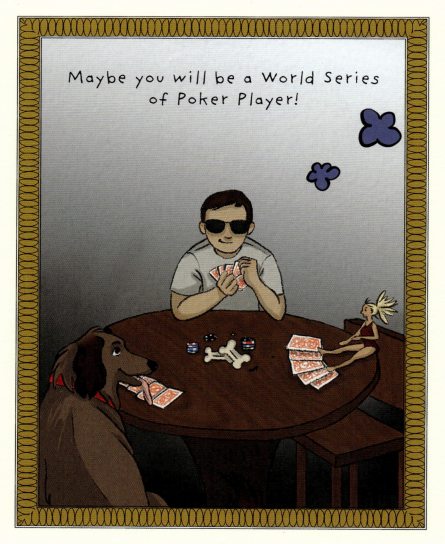

... or maybe you *will* be losing your money to on-line poker at night while working at the DMV by day.

Career Fun Facts:

- Most professional poker players have 401(k) type retirement funds that involve the words "scratch off."

- Not all people that work at the Department of Motor Vehicles are negative and rude. Just those that have been working there for over a week.

- Percentage of professional poker players that do not go bankrupt: 3.7%.

- Number of on-line poker players: over 40,000,000.

- Number of on-line poker players who are happily married: 2 (and they are married to each other).

- Poker is the most televised event on *ESPN!* (Seriously).

... or maybe you will be a production assistant in a not-so-reputable movie.

Career Fun Facts:
- The male Brown Antechinus (type of mouse) has a two-week mating season and will mate as many times as possible during that period. It has been known to get it on for up to fourteen hours straight! This is termed by scientists as "suicidal reproduction" as it will often result in his death.

- When the male honey bee mates, his pecker is ripped off and his balls explode, thus resulting in his untimely death. Don't believe it? Look it up.

... or maybe you *will* participate in a competitive eating contest.

Career Fun Facts:
- Percentage of competitive eaters who have a shred of dignity: 0.00%.

- Percentage of competitive eaters who will live past the age of 35: 3%.

- Percentage of people whose gag reflex is triggered by witnessing a hot dog eating contest: 42%.

- Vomiting is commonly known as "reversals" during a hot dog eating contest.

- Writing about "reversals" just now made me sick to my stomach.

- While training, the average contestant defecates enough to fill a kitchen crock-pot daily.

... or maybe you will be a barnyard masturbator.

Career Fun Facts:

-This is really a job!

-Barnyard masturbator was ranked as the third worst job in science by Popular Science Magazine.

-17% of semen collectors have suffered a perforated eardrum due to the cacophonous shrills of the beasts as they reach climax.

-Left-handed men are typically more ambidextrous and can readily masturbate with either hand, while right-handed men are likely to rupture a testicle should they try to "switch it up."

-The highest stud fee for an American stallion is Tapit at $300,000 per insemination. He earns nearly $12.6 million per year. I will save you the time- that's 42 "trips to the plate!"

-The stimulation device used for bulls is known as a "rectal electrifier."

... or maybe you will be the one who starts the fires.

Career Fun Facts:
- Every boy likes to play with fire. I repeat, EVERY boy likes to play with fire! Mom, don't freak out if your son is torching his army men.

- According to the two police officers surveyed, 100% of firefighters are gay.

- Number of "suspicious" fires started every year: 4.1 million.

- Number of ants that perish every year due to "spontaneous" magnifying glass combustion: 7.4 billion.

... or maybe you will be an overly competitive Pee Wee football coach.

Career Fun Facts:
-All coaches were exceptional athletes in their youth. Don't believe it? Just ask one.

-The odds of a high school senior football player making the NFL is nine in ten-thousand (0.09%). Ironically, those are the same odds of a mom liking this book.

-Yelling at and demeaning a child is the best way to build character; provided you are trying to develop an alcoholic, abusive, and maladjusted adult.

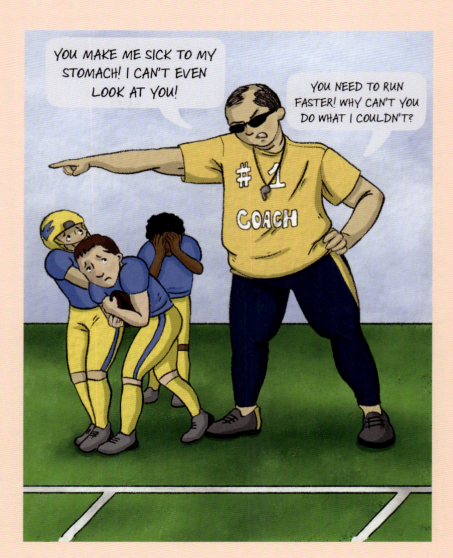

... or maybe you will end up contracting a rare tropical disease.

Career Fun Facts:
 -Biomedical scientists rank third in suicide rates by profession, behind dentists and authors of demeaning satirical books.

 -Julius "Doctor J" Erving was not really a doctor. He does not have a medical or doctorate degree and left college early to play professional basketball. He later earned a bachelor's degree from the University of Massachusetts Amherst in 1986. Good for him.

... or maybe your "job" will be gaming with your "friends."

Career Fun Facts:
- Most professional gamers don't date because it takes away from their craft. Yeah, that's the reason.

- Mountain Dew Code Red and Nacho Cheese Doritos contain many of the necessary vitamins and minerals for a complete balanced diet... as well as a whole lot of shit that can swell your prostate to the size of a fist.

- Percentage of 13 year-old boys who list "video game designing" as a potential career path: 54%.

- Number of employed video game designers: 65,678.

- Number of gamers prepping for the job: 1.244 billion.

- Odds of success in this career path: 0.000053%

- Odds of alienating every member of your family while pursuing your "career": 100%.

... or maybe you will be a really fast Uber driver.

Career Fun Facts:
-An Uber/Lyft driver only drives because he wants to meet people and pick up a few extra bucks to supplement his six-figure job at the investment house. At least that's what every driver tells me.

-23% of male drivers keep an empty Gatorade bottle under their seat to urinate in between rides.

-7% admit to using the bottle for something significantly more disgusting.

-Uber drivers do not need to pass a drug test.

-You are only required to have a license for one year to be an Uber driver.

... or maybe you will nurse... a lot.

Career Fun Facts:
- We told you moms would hate this book, so why are you shaking your head right now?

- 2.54% of nursing mothers can squirt milk up to 20 feet.

- Fireball Cinnamon Whiskey is the number one "go-to" shot in most bars.

- Some women have been known to breastfeed their children to an excess of nine years of age.

... or maybe you will be a stalker.

Career Fun Facts:
- Percentage of people who think they are photographers because their phone has a camera: 98%.

- Number of men in the world: 3,776,294,273.

- Number of stalkers in the world: 3,776,294,272.

- One of the authors is NOT a stalker.

- Women, if you know someone that has a crush on you and you think he's harmless, HE'S NOT! (By the way, I think you're very pretty).

... or maybe you will be the president of your homeowner's association.

Career Fun Facts:
 -Do not try to make your HOA President happy. It cannot be done.

-HOA Presidents are sadistic, power-hungry, inconsiderate, ungrateful, sexually frustrated, sad excuses of whale shit. (Sorry, I had a bad experience.)

-Over 1.1 million Americans have a reverse mortgage and a few of them do not regret it!

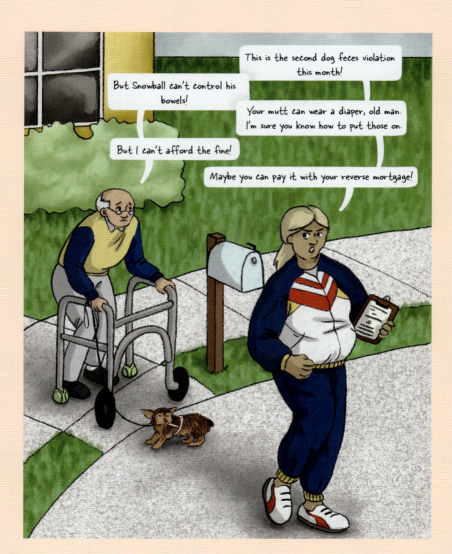

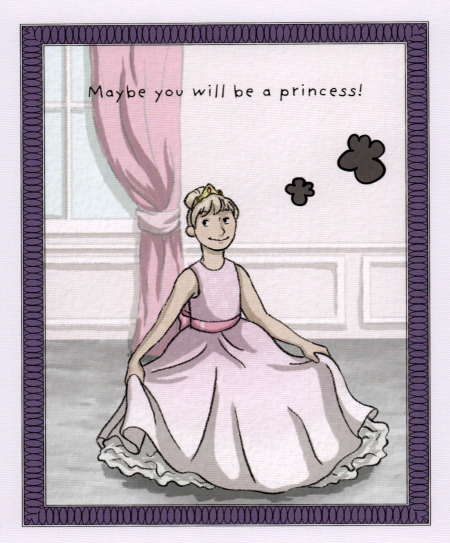

... or maybe your stage name will be "Princess."

Career Fun Facts:
- Snow White was fourteen years old. Does that make Prince Ferdinand a pedophile!?

- Carrie Fisher did not like the revealing Princess Leia outfit in the Return of the Jedi. It worked for this Star Wars fan!

- Not all fraternities exploit women. Oh, wait. Yes, they do.

... or maybe you *will* be eaten by a remote Amazonian tribe.

Career Fun Facts:
 - Number of people who die annually from cannibalism: no idea, but one seems like too many.

 - Cannibals are known for being very efficient with using the entire body. Commonly, human skin is used for canoe building and the bones are formed into tools, weapons, and very fancy jewelry!

 -100% of all missionaries die from issues that may or may not relate to their work with missions. That is a fact!

... or maybe you will close your own restaurant.

Career Fun Facts:
- Most restaurants open in buildings that were previously restaurants that went out of business. Think about that.

- Percentage of non-franchised restaurant start-ups that fail within the first five years: 94%
(but I'm sure YOU will be in the 6%!).

- The best way to have a restaurant worth one million dollars is to invest two million... and wait twelve months.

- Everybody that works at your restaurant will steal from you. EVERYBODY! When a bartender or server says, "this one's on me"... it's not.

- 77% of start-up restaurants owned by women fail in the first year.

- 23% of start-up restaurants owned by men succeed in the first year.

... or maybe you will just sing karaoke on the nursing home circuit.

Career Fun Facts:
- Michael Jackson's "Billie Jean" is the most requested song for karaoke.

- When a group of drunk girls get up to sing karaoke "Love Shack", LEAVE IMMEDIATELY.

- If you think you are a good karaoke singer, you aren't. You are awful. If you think you are bad, you are right and why did you get up to sing?

... or maybe you will end up on Times Square "portraying" a superhero.

Career Fun Facts:
-Real superheroes are police officers, fire fighters, military personnel, and Seth MacFarlane.

-If you ever take a picture with a character in Times Square it is recommended you do not touch their costume. You will likely be itching for a while.

-Robert John Burck, the original Naked Cowboy, ran for President of the United States as a Tea Party candidate.

... or maybe you should look at your gene pool.

Career Fun Facts:
- Just because you are skinny does not mean you are a super model... and you are not that skinny.

- Mom, do not get your daughter started with pageants. She is not that cute.

- Most supermodels eat whatever they want, whenever they want. (Provided they purge shortly thereafter).

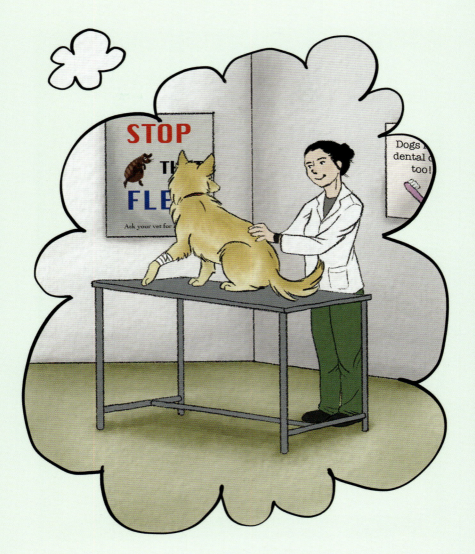

... or maybe you will be the person who picks up roadkill.

Career Fun Facts:

-The job of an animal renderer is to collect roadkill and dead animals from farms and recycle them into more useful materials, such as lard or tallow. Over 43,000 people work in the rendering industry in the United States!

-In most states, you can be placed on a call list to pick-up "fresh-kill" animals.

-The majority of fat in rendered road kill is used as a skin-conditioning agent and an emollient in cosmetics such as lipstick, eyeshadow, and soap.

-The average human that regularly eats at a Chinese buffet could produce in excess of 450 bars of bath soap.

-The average cost for a professional burial of a cat is between $400-$600. Amazon sells shovels for less than $11.

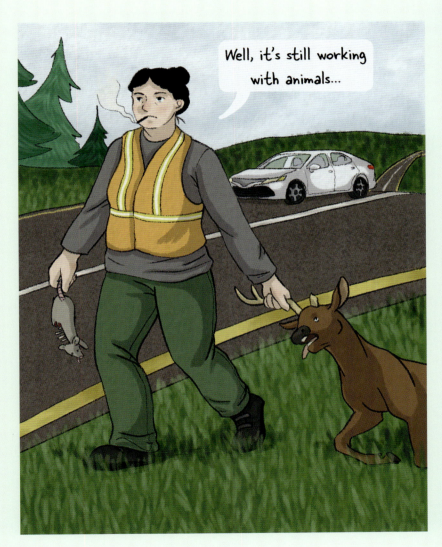

...or maybe you will police the Space Mountain fast-pass line at Disney's Magic Kingdom.

Career Fun Facts:
- The first original character created by Walt Disney was a rabbit called Oswald the Lucky Rabbit.

- There is at least 10% rat hair in every mouse ear cap.

- We are joking! Disney, please do not sue us.

- It's actually 30%.

- Every Disney employee is required to fabricate a stupid, painted-on, condescending smile... like that of Mickey Mouse!

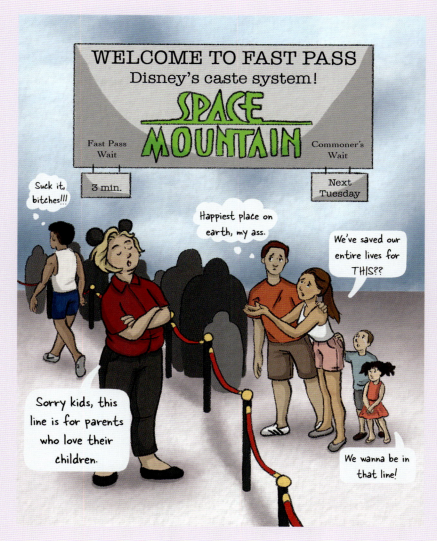

... or maybe you will be an "exotic" dancer.

Yep... we went there again.

Career Fun Facts:
- I saw the Nutcracker and HATED IT!

- Strippers can write-off breast implants as a tax deduction. (Be sure to consult your tax advisor).

- Strippers make more money when ovulating. (Seriously).

- England's Royal Ballet troupe goes through approximately 15,000 pairs of pointe shoes a year!

- 7% of strippers are married... 100% of their husbands are unemployed.

- The inside of toe-shoes smell like burnt toast. (Of course that's not true. Why would you believe that?)

- Moms, why are you still reading this book?

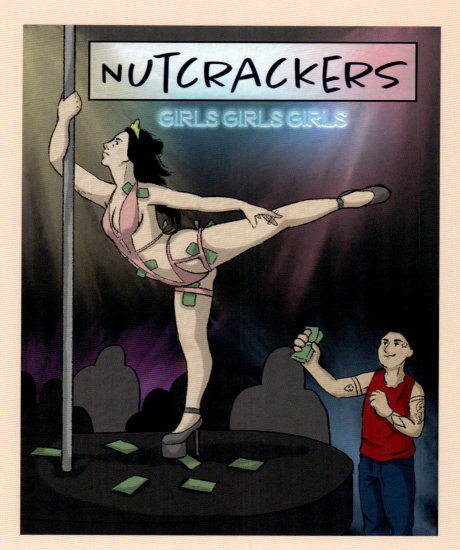

... or maybe you will be someone who likes to argue with everyone instead.

Career Fun Facts:
- 36% of American Attorneys have a drinking problem.

- Percentage of attorneys and accountants who GREATLY pad their billable hours: I'm not sure, but I'm thinking 100%.

- Percentage of statistics that are typically fabricated: 86.2%... including this one (plus or minus a standard deviation of 3%).

- 100% of the fun facts in this book are either factual or fabricated by the authors.

- If you are an attorney and reading this, not the career you thought it would be, huh?

... or maybe you will realize too late that the "children's book" you illustrate is not what it was cracked up to be.

Maybe this book will be successful... or maybe it won't!

Final Fun Fact:

My parents are still angry about this.

This book was truly a collaborative effort. Significant credit goes to the following:

Tony Lamb

Allen Griffith

Danny Reynolds

Evan Reynolds

Karen Schultz

Elizabeth Kluthe Lachmann

Tim Miller

Josh Bornhorn

Jason Gray

and several others...